Look After Yourself

Healthy Food

Angela Royston

Heinemann Library
Chicago, Illinois

Designed by Dave Oakley
Photo research by Helen Reilly
Originated by Dot Gradations Ltd
Printed and bound in China by South China Printing Company

07 06 05 04 03
10 9 8 7 6 5 4 3 2 1

Library of Congress Cataloging-in-Publication Data
Royston, Angela.
Healthy food / Angela Royston.
v. cm. -- (Look after yourself)
Includes bibliographical references and index.
Contents: Your body -- Eating -- Eat all kinds of food -- A balance for good health -- Starchy foods -- Fruits and vegetables -- Fiber -- Food that help you grow -- Milk -- Fight the fat -- Sugar attack! -- Water -- It's a fact.
ISBN 1-4034-4439-0 (libr. bdg.) -- ISBN 1-4034-4448-X (pbk.)
1. Nutrition--Juvenile literature. [1. Nutrition.] I. Title.
RA784.R698 2003
613.2--dc21
2003000995

Acknowledgments
The author and publisher are grateful to the following for permission to reproduce copyright material:
Cover photograph by Hein Van den Heuvel/Zefa/BP.
pp. 4, 5, 6, 7, 9, 14, 15, 16, 17, 21, 24, 27 Trevor Clifford; p. 8 S. Grant/Trip; pp. 11, 12, 18, 22 Photodisc; p. 13 Corbis; p. 19 Zarember/Trip; p. 20 Powerstock; p. 23 Claire Paxton/Bubbles; p. 25 Chester/Trip; p. 26 Science Photo Library.

Special thanks to David Wright for his help in the preparation of this book.

Every effort has been made to contact copyright holders of any material reproduced in this book. Any omissions will be rectified in subsequent printings if notice is given to the publisher.

Some words are shown in bold, **like this.** You can find out what they mean by looking in the glossary.

Contents

Your Body

Your body is like a complicated machine.
Most machines need fuel to keep them going.
Car engines burn gasoline to make them work.
Food is your body's fuel.

Your body uses food to make **energy.** Different kinds of food help keep your body machine going strong.

Eating

Before your body can use food, the food has to be broken down into tiny pieces. Your teeth, tongue, and mouth chew food into small pieces.

When you **swallow,** food moves down into your stomach. Here, the food is broken down into even smaller pieces that your body can use.

Eat All Kinds of Foods

It is good to eat food that you enjoy, but make sure you eat all kinds of foods. Different kinds of foods help your body in different ways.

If you never eat fruit or vegetables, for example, your body will not work so well. Eating different kinds of foods keeps your body healthy.

A Balance for Good Health

Your body needs more of some kinds of foods than others. If you eat foods from each of these food groups, you are eating a **balanced diet.**

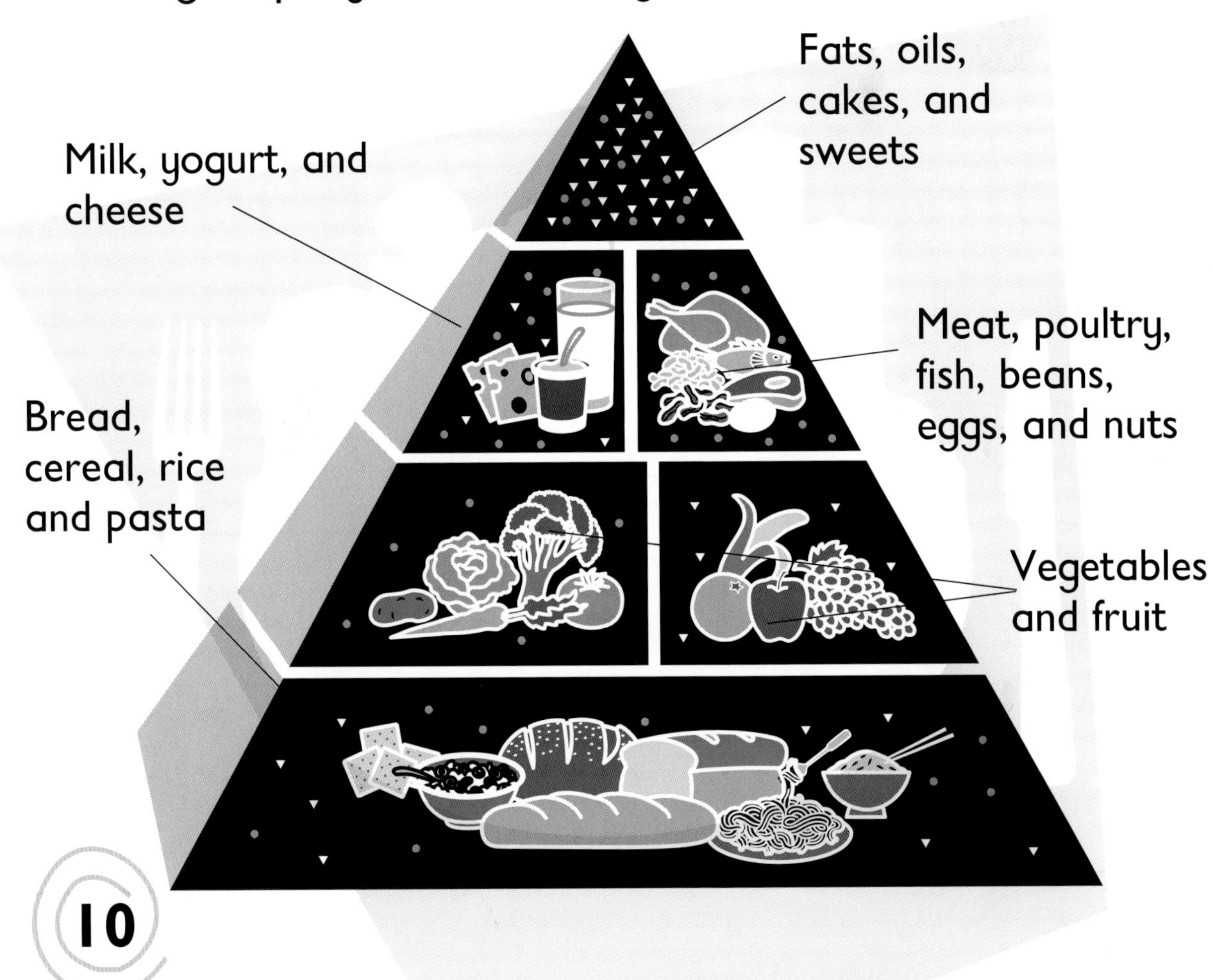

Your body needs more of the foods shown at the bottom of the **pyramid** on page ten. You should eat less of the foods shown at the top.

Starchy Foods

Starch gives you **energy.** These foods are all full of starch. Make sure you eat one or more starchy foods at every meal.

Your body uses energy all the time. When you run around, your muscles use lots of energy. But even sitting still, your body uses energy.

Fruits and Vegetables

Fruits and vegetables contain lots of **vitamins** and **minerals.** These are things that help your body work properly. Other foods contain some vitamins and minerals, too.

Each vitamin and mineral helps your body in a different way. Some minerals make your bones strong. Some vitamins make your skin healthy.

Fiber

Fruits and vegetables contain something called **fiber.** Potato skins, **whole grain** bread, and other foods contain fiber, too. This sandwich on whole wheat bread has lots of fiber.

Fiber from food passes through your body. Fiber helps your body get rid of waste.

Foods That Help You Grow

These foods all contain a lot of **protein.** You should eat two or three servings of this kind of food every day. Most **starchy** foods contain some protein, too.

eggs

fish

beans

nuts

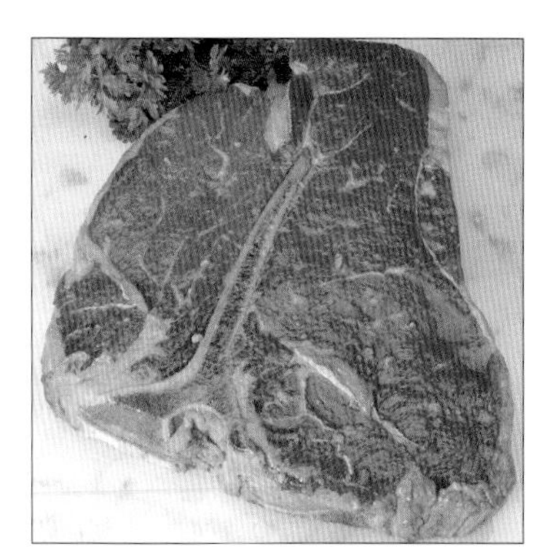

meat

Every part of your body is made mainly of protein. You need to eat protein in food to help your body grow bigger and taller.

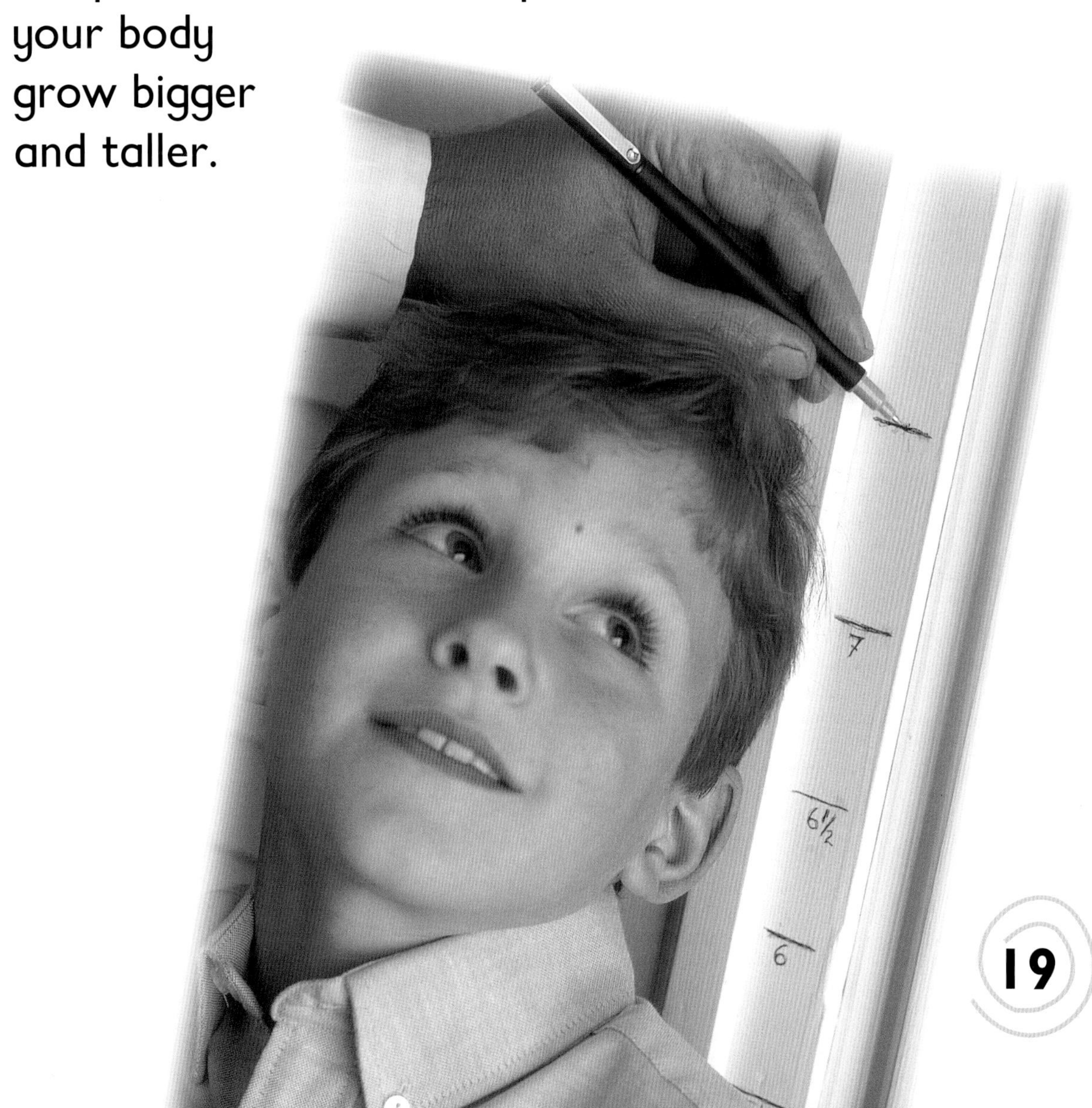

Milk

Milk contains a **mineral** called **calcium.** This mineral makes your bones and teeth strong and hard. You should drink milk every day.

Cheese and yogurt contain calcium, too. Some of them are made from cows' milk. Others are made from goats' milk or sheep's milk.

Fight the Fat

Foods like these contain a lot of fat. Fat gives you some **energy,** like **starch** does. Your body also uses fat to stay warm.

Your body stores extra fat in a layer under your skin. If you eat too much fat, your body will store up too much This can make you gain weight.

Sugar Attack!

Many drinks and foods contain a lot of sugar. Sugar tastes sweet and gives you **energy.** But too much sugar is not good for your body or your teeth.

When you eat or drink sweet things, some sugar stays in your mouth. This sugar can hurt your teeth. Try to brush your teeth after you eat or drink anything sweet.

Water

Your body needs lots of water to stay healthy. You lose water as you **sweat** and when you go to the bathroom.

You should drink about five or six cups of liquid a day to replace the water you lose. All drinks are mainly water. Some foods also contain water. Try to choose drinks like unsweetened juices and plain water.

It's a Fact!

Some people are allergic to certain foods. This means that when they eat them, their body reacts as if they are sick. They may get sick, their mouth may swell up, or they may get a rash on their skin.

People who are allergic to cows' milk sometimes drink **soy milk** or goats' milk instead. They can also get some **calcium** by eating **okra,** broccoli, **sardines,** or white bread.

The healthiest drink is clean water. Water helps your body break down food. Drinking some milk and pure fruit juice is also good for your body, because they contain **vitamins** and **minerals.**

Drinks sweetened with sugar can hurt your teeth. These drinks include lemonade, cola, and fruit sodas.

Eating or drinking sugary things may give you a quick burst of **energy,** but it does not last. Soon, you feel more tired than before you had the sugar. The energy you get from eating **starch** lasts much longer.

You can live for more than a week without food, but only a few days without water.

Your stomach stores food for up to four hours.

Waste food can take more than a whole day and night to pass through your body.

Glossary

balanced diet eating a mixture of many foods, but especially foods containing fiber, proteins, and starches

calcium mineral that makes your teeth and bones strong and hard

energy power to do work or move about

fiber parts of plants that the body cannot digest and that pass right through the body

mineral chemical that is contained in some foods and that your body needs to stay healthy

okra kind of vegetable that consists of a sticky green pod and seeds

protein chemicals in food that help your body grow

pyramid square base with four triangular sides that meet at a point

sardine small sea fish

soy milk milk that is made from soybeans

starch substance that gives the body energy. Bread, pasta, potatoes, and rice are starchy foods.

swallow push food from your mouth down your throat

sweat salty water that the body makes in the skin, particularly when you are hot

vitamin chemical that is contained in some foods and that your body needs to stay healthy

whole grain foods made from some plants in which the outer layer of the grain has not been taken off

More Books to Read

Royston, Angela. *Eat Well.* Chicago: Heinemann Library, 1999.

Spilsbury, Louise. *Milk.* Chicago: Heinemann Library, 2001.

Vogel, Elizabeth. *Eating Right.* New York: PowerKids Press, 2001.

Index